Published by Center Avenue Media

ISBN-13: 978-1523699421
ISBN-10: 1523699426

THRIVE.

A Workbook to Help Your Family's
Finances Thrive in Today's Economy.

THRIVE

When I was in junior high, my mom would take my younger sister, brother, and I to the grocery store on Saturday mornings to help choose what would go in our lunches at school. I remember our family's weekly grocery budget—$100—because we carefully estimated each item that went into our cart. Often, having Oreos in our lunch at school hinged on what coupons we could find in the *Chicago Tribune* circulars that week.

Today, I am a father of two toddlers, and groceries take a significant bite out of our family's budget. My three and four year old aren't shucking oysters or choosing from an assortment of aged cheeses: they eat cooked noodles, chicken, and anything else that can be dipped in ketchup or ranch dressing. But packing healthy snacks and feeding them natural foods adds up quickly. High-quality meat, milk that's free from antibiotics or hormones, and fruits and vegetables that aren't treated with harmful chemicals are premium products—and even though the science behind GMO's and Organics is debatable, we make every effort to feed our children natural foods because we believe that's what's best for them. Feeding children healthy food shouldn't be a luxury we're thankful we can afford.

Our grocery bill's growing appetite is just one way our family, like millions of others in this country, has felt the pressure of an increased cost of living over the past decade. The increasing disproportionality between what people make and the cost of raising a family has affected more than people's access to healthy food: it's made us dependent on unhealthy financial habits, too.

Survival of the Financially Fittest

Over the last 10 years, it's become more expensive to raise a family. While household income has increased by roughly 26% in the past 12 years, the cost of living has gone up 29%, with necessities like food, housing, and medical care significantly outpacing income growth.[1] A few things, like gasoline, have gotten cheaper, but the majority of the goods and services that

Income (not Adjusted for Inflation) Versus the Cost of Living in the US[1]

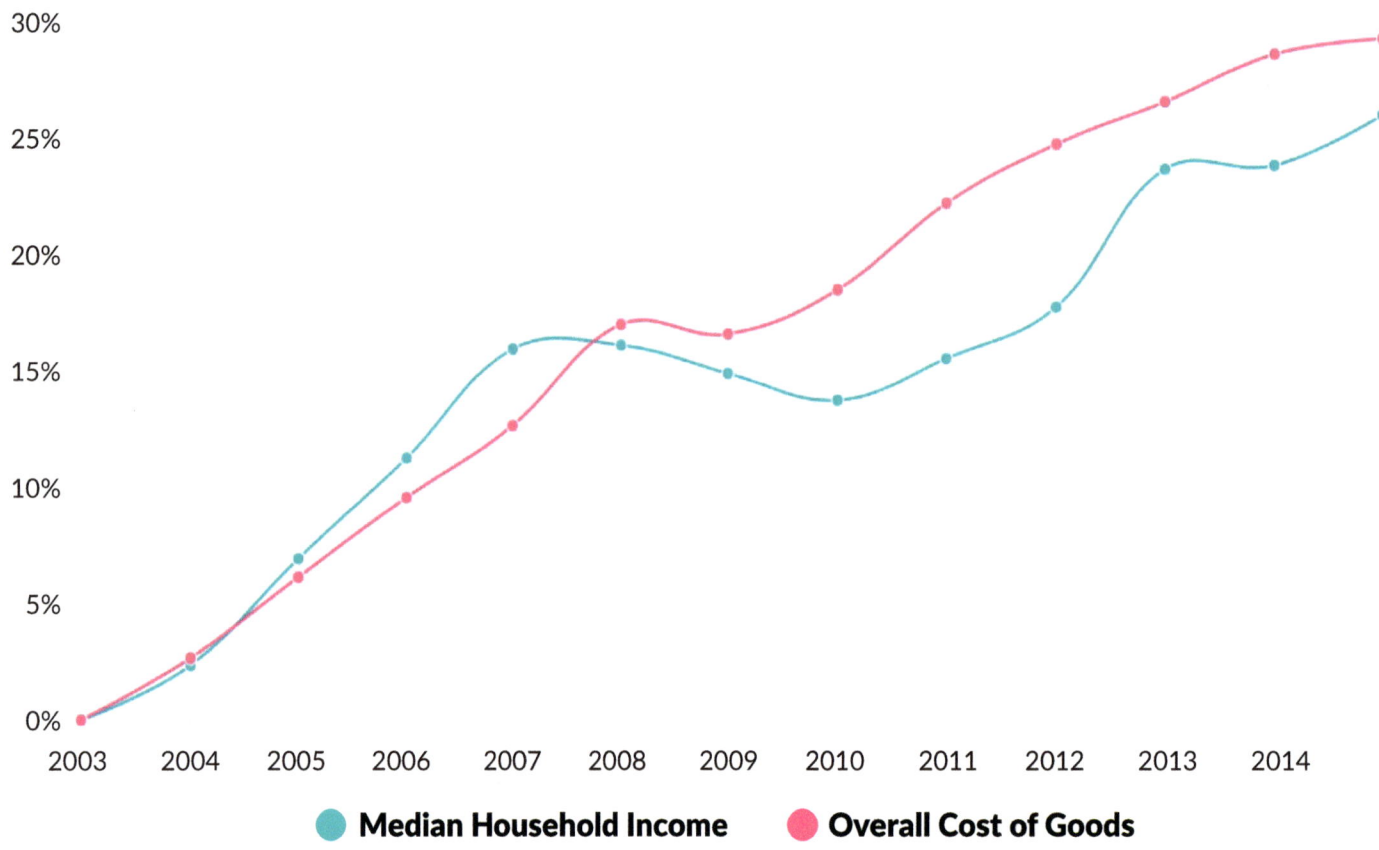

Median Household Income **Overall Cost of Goods**

make up your family's budget have become more costly than ever. Low unemployment numbers and an increasing GDP can be misleading, as they appear to signal a recovery from the financial crisis of 2008[2]; however, most peoples' wages haven't been able to keep pace with an increasing cost of living.

Most people's wages haven't been able to keep up with and increasing cost of living. As a result, more households have turned to financing, causing household debt to outpace income by 15% since 2003[1].

Thriving Financially as a Family in America after 2008

An increased cost of living and rapidly accumulating debt aren't the only challenges facing many families in America today. The financial crisis of 2008 left a wake of foreclosures, short sales, and lost wages that wiped out the savings of millions of American families. Many more people were left with mortgage balances that far exceeded the new value of their homes.

Fluctuating markets have all but eliminated some peoples' entire savings, strained local and state budgets have drained the pension savings of police, firefighters, and teachers, and home values are still languishing in most areas of the country, as foreclosures still plague many neighborhoods.

Traditional investments like retirement accounts, public pensions, and home equity are no longer the same reliable source of financial stability that they once were.

Debt Owed by U.S. Households and Comsumers[1]

	TOTAL OWED BY AVG. U.S. HOUSEHOLD	TOTAL DEBT OWED BY U.S. CONSUMERS
Credit Cards	$15,355	$712 billion
Mortgages	$165,892	$8.12 trillion
Auto Loans	$26,530	$1.03 trillion
Student Loans	$47,712	$1.21 trillion
Any Type of Debt	$129,579	$11.91 trillion

The average household pays a total of $6,658 in interest per year.

Given the challenging economic circumstances a young family faces today, finding financial success might seem nearly impossible - especially for families with children. With so many expenses— food, clothes, childcare, to name a few— it's easy to lose track of your family's spending.

Your family's ability to thrive in today's economy requires financial fitness—the ability to actively manage income in order to avoid debt, save money, and grow wealth.

It's not about how much you *make*: it's about how you *manage* it.

According to a recent study by the US Department of Agriculture, the cost of raising a child born in 2013 (from birth to age 18) is estimated to be a staggering $245,340.[3] On a more immediate level, Parents can count on spending close to $50 per week ($2,448 per year) on diapers, formula and baby food alone.[4] This number doesn't account for things larger expenses like daycare or education, either. There's simply no way around it: the cost of raising a child has a massive impact on any family's budget.

It's no wonder many people have chosen to put off starting a family as they accumulate record amounts of student debt and struggle to find living-wage jobs. This growing trend is just one of the ways that we're all beginning to see how finances today are different than they were a generation ago.

There's no doubt that there has been a significant shift in how families must manage their finances in order to afford healthy food, live comfortably, save for college, and prepare for retirement. And while the traditional means of investing aren't as predictable as they once were for previous generations, they are based on sound principles—smart saving and responsible spending—that are still every bit as effective.

This book is designed for families who aren't content with merely surviving from one paycheck to the next without the security of a significant savings account or long-term plan for affording college and retirement.

In the coming pages, you'll learn 6 important principles that can help ensure your family's financial health in today's American economy.

Families are an essential part of the American fabric and fundamental to the economic engine that drives our country. Families have a strong association with economic growth: there is a direct correlation between families that thrive and the communities in which they live.[5]

What It Means to **THRIVE**

The 6 principles of the **THRIVE** approach to family finance are based on sound, basic fundamentals like budgeting, saving, and making both long and short-term investments. In short, it's a common sense approach to carefully monitoring and managing your family's finances.

THRIVE begins with setting an important short and long-term goal: to repair, improve, or maintain your credit score. Because your credit score is the key indicator of your family's financial health, it's essential to understand, monitor, and work hard to improve it. Your credit score probably impacts you in more ways than you know. Not only does your credit score determine your ability to borrow money (through credit cards and fixed-term loans), it is used to calculate interest rates, the cost of your auto insurance, and even the deposit you're required to have on file with many utility companies.

While **THRIVE** does call for fiscal discipline, it's not intended to put families in an uncomfortable position, either. **THRIVE** is a balanced approach to managing your family's spending habits that is designed to help you live more comfortably after getting your finances in shape.

Thriving means more than just spending smart and saving money. It requires hard work to establish healthy financial habits, but, in the end, results in more financial freedom and security.

The 6 Principles of THRIVE

T **H** **R** **I** **V** **E**

| THOROUGHLY EXAMINE SPENDING | HAVE AN EMERGENCY FUND | REDUCE DEBT | INVEST AND INSURE | VISIT YOUR ACCOUNTS OFTEN | ENJOY FINANCIAL FREEDOM |

1. Thoroughly Examine Your Spending

The first step in getting your finances in order is to conduct some research in the form of account statements.

2. Have an Emergency Fund

Before paying down your debt, you'll learn some creative ways to set aside your first $1,000 in a "rainy day" fund.

3. Reduce Debt

Through a systematic approach, you'll consolidate debt, reduce what you're paying in interest, and accelerate your payments.

4. Invest and Insure

It's never too early to start investing - even if it's a small amount. Having the proper insurance coverage is also an essential investment.

5. Visit Your Accounts Often

Today, there are many tools available to help you monitor your accounts. You'll learn how to keep an eye on scheduled payments, pending charges, and cash flow.

6. Enjoy Financial Freedom

After getting your finances organized and formulating a plan, you'll be able to find many ways to enjoy your new-found financial freedom.

Short-Term Strategy, Long-Term Payoff

Your family's finances are a lot like your health. If you don't watch what you eat and maintain a balanced diet, your unhealthy habits will eventually catch up with you—and the results can be catastrophic.

Maintaining a healthy diet requires you to be attentive, disciplined, and have a lot of patience. Regular exercise, wholesome foods, and balanced nutrition all help keep many chronic conditions under control.

Just like a diabetic needs to carefully monitor his blood sugar, or a person with a gluten intolerance must watch what she eats, you'll be keeping close tabs on the money that comes in and out of each of your accounts.

It's no simple task to balance your family's growing needs with your finances: however, without paying careful attention to the many bills, loans, fees, and investment opportunities, your family's finances are at risk of getting very, very out of shape.

Start by setting some short and long-term goals—there's no heavy lifting just yet. Then, we'll move on to the first principle of THRIVE: Thoroughly Examine Your Spending.

30 YEARS

Write down one financial goal you have 30 years from today:

----

15 YEARS

Write down one financial goal you have 15 years from today:

----

10 YEARS

Write down one financial goal you have 10 years from today:

----

1 YEAR

Write down one financial goal you have 1 year from today:

T Thoroughly Examine Your Spending

Family finances are complex. There's a tricky balance of bills and accounts (the average person has 3.7 credit cards[5]), and it can be very confusing to miss a due date, as they probably all fall on different days each month. This ever-changing calendar of payments can easily become complicated, causing you to miss a payment or, even worse, forget about an account entirely.

Pull a Credit Report

The only way to really know for sure which accounts are open in your name is to run a credit report. You don't have to run an official report, which results in a "hard inquiry" and, consequently counts against your score: you can use a website like Credit Karma and check it for free. The site will give you an accurate listing of all of your accounts, both current and former. If you spot any suspicious balances or open lines of credit, or if you see any activity that looks fraudulent, you should report it to your bank immediately.

Passwords

Almost every one of your accounts can be managed online (many companies even offer incentives for "going paperless"). But with each new account comes a new password, and, with each password, a new set of rules pertaining to length, capitalization, and special characters. Determine a secure place to keep all of your usernames and passwords organized.

For your convenience, we've included a technology-proof storage solution at the end of this book. A hand-written list is also easy for family members to access in an emergency.

☐ **Conduct a "soft" credit inquiry online (for free).**

☐ **List your accounts at the end of this book. Recover/reset any lost passwords and write them down.**

8 Ways to Cut Your Family's Monthly Spending

ASK FOR BETTER RATES OR PRICES

Sometimes, getting a better rate or a discount is simply a matter of asking. Call your credit card company, bank, or TV provider and see if they'll be willing to extend a promotional rate.

CANCEL CLUB MEMBERSHIPS

Look into cutting gym memberships and other monthly subscriptions out of your budget. If you're not sure you can cancel because paid in advance, ask about a credit or refund.

REDUCE OR ELIMINATE SERVICES

Cord-cutting is all the rage - and with services like Netflix and Hulu, it's easy to access to TV and Movies.

FIND INEXPENSIVE ENTERTAINMENT

Look for parks, local museums, and park district programs. Most communities have affordable options for families with children of all ages.

REDUCE/ELIMINATE ALCOHOL & SMOKING

If you're buying cigarettes and alchohol, you're burning through your budget without much to show for it. Skip the six pack and stash the cash instead.

STOP GOING OUT TO EAT

Stopping for coffee or grabbing take-out will really take a bite out of your family budget. Brew a pot of coffee instead of stopping for a Latte in the morning.

LOOK FOR CHEAPER CHILD CARE

Consider reducing the number of days you're sending the kids to day care. Also, look for a nanny share or consider enlisting the help of a family member or friend.

GET A NEW QUOTE FOR INSURANCE

Shopping around for a better rate will likely save you money - especially if you're able to combine your auto policy with another policy from the

Statements

Once you've listed your accounts, usernames, and passwords, log in to each of your accounts and download all of your statements from the previous 3 months You probably don't need to go further back than that, because most of your family's expenses are monthly. However, some utilities are billed bi-monthly or even quarterly, and it's essential to keep them in consideration.

Comb over the statements to determine what your family spends each month on fixed costs, such as your mortgage or rent, car payment, student loan payments, and other services (like your cell phone or cable service/internet provider).

Next, you can use the last three months' statements to calculate, on average, what your family spends each month on items that fluctuate, like food, gas, and entertainment, as well as utilities like electricity and water.

Once you've got a clear picture of what your family is spending each month, you'll also likely be able to see some areas where you can cut back or even eliminate wasteful spending. If your spending is break even, and you're not saving much, it's worth taking a closer look at what you can cut. If your spending is negative—you're spending a little more each month than you make—it's time to decide which expenses you're willing to eliminate.

Trimming Your Expenses

Deciding where to cut back on spending isn't easy. And, if you're going to do it in an impactful way, it will probably require you to make some sacrifices in the short term. If you're carrying a balance on your credit cards each month, it's probably costing you more than you think. If your spending is hindering your ability to pay down debt—or if you're routinely using a credit card and paying interest on these expenses—it's time for some serious consideration about where to cut costs.

Trimming your expenses is a necessary step that comes before eliminating credit card debt, building up your savings, and investing at least a little each month for college and retirement.

☐ **Complete the chart to the right to find out what you're spending each month—and what you're willing to do to save some money.**

ITEM/SERVICE	MONTHLY SPENDING (how much you spend each month)	WAYS TO SAVE (check the things you're willing or able to do)
DINING OUT		☐ Eliminate Dining Out ☐ Limit Dining Out to 1x Each Month ☐ Brew Coffee at Home
CREDIT CARD FEES		☐ Consolidate Credit Cards to a no-interest Card ☐ Ask your bank for a reduction in fees
LAWN SERVICE		☐ Reduce the frequency of your lawn service ☐ Eliminate lawn service
INTERNET		☐ Shop around for a cheaper plan ☐ Ask your carrier for a better rate ☐ Accept a slower connection speed
PHONE		☐ Reduce you data useage/plan ☐ Shop around for another carrier ☐ Ask your carrier for a discount/better rate ☐ Don't get a new phone when your plan expires
CABLE/SATELLITE		☐ Shop around for another carrier ☐ Ask your carrier for a discount/better rate ☐ Downgrade your programming package ☐ Cancel premium chanels ☐ Switch to Netflix or Hulu for programming
ENTERTAINMENT		☐ Find free or low-cost options in your community ☐ Cancel subscription services (Apple Music, Spotify)
GYM MEMBERSHIP		☐ Join a less expensive gym ☐ Ask your gym for a better rate or discount ☐ Cancel your membership
GROCERIES		☐ Purchase generic, store-brand items ☐ Find and use coupons ☐ Adjust your diet ☐ Buy some commodities in bulk (CostCo, Sams)
ACTIVITIES		☐ Utilize Park District programs ☐ Eliminate some or all private lessons or programs
CHILDCARE		☐ Find and join a nanny share ☐ Find and join a babysitting co-op ☐ Seek out more affordable daycare

Ⓗ Have an Emergency Fund

Once you've determined which things you're willing to cut back on each month, you've set the stage for good spending habits. Your finances won't improve overnight, though – it's going take time and patience before you see the effects of your new spending habits. In the meantime, let's stash some money nearby to help cover your unexpected ER visit or insurance deductible.

A good number to start with is $1,000. This should be enough to cover most unexpected expenses, including medical co-payments, insurance deductibles, and emergency repairs.

If your budget is already maxed out, here are a few ways to build up your emergency fund:

- Sell some things on eBay, Craigslist, or other neighborhood network

- Take on a part-time gig, like tutoring or babysitting

- Sell goods or digital services on an online marketplace like Etsy or Fiverr.

Your emergency fund is essential to your success at achieving financial freedom. Without it, you're at risk of charging unforeseen expenses to your credit card—and getting stuck with paying the interest on a balance that carries over. Because **THRIVE** depends on eliminating high-interest borrowing in order to maintain healthy credit, an emergency fund is not optional. If tap into this fund, it's essential to rebuild it as soon as possible.

☐ **Find some creative ways to raise and save $1,000. Keep it somewhere safe, and only use this money for an emergency.**

7 Common Emergencies

and what you can expect to pay for them

	EXPENSE	AVERAGE COST
	Emergency Room Visit (Deductibles, Co-Pays, etc.)[6]	$1,233
	Auto Accident Insurance Decutible[7]	$500
	Auto Repair[8]	$367.84
	In-State Move[9]	$1,170
	Plane Ticket for Last-Minute, Emergency Travel[10]	$379
	Furnance Repair[11]	$267
	Replace Water Heater (Including Plumbing Costs)[12]	$4,000

Ⓡ Reduce Your Debt

As a general rule, debt is bad for families. High interest rates can cause balances to grow exponentially in a short time, and you should avoid charging anything to your credit cards that you won't be paying off at the end of the month.

There are some exceptions. Sometimes, it's nessecary—or maybe even to your advantage—to go into debt. It makes sense when going into debt brings in more than the interest you'll pay. Consider a home mortgage loan with a low interest rate. If you're borrowing $200k at 4%, and your home value appreciates at a greater rate, you're leveraging your borrowing ability to get a positive return on your investment. Obtaining a certification or relocating for a higher-paying job might come at a considerable near-term cost that requires financing, but the trade-off might be a higher salary later.

The better your credit score is, the lower interest rate you'll be charged. And even in circumstances that do require financing, it's important to avoid using credit cards if you won't be able to pay the balance in full at the end of the month.

Take a look at the example of what just one credit card that carries a $1,000 balance might cost in just one month. Because credit cards compound, you'll be charged interest on the interest if you don't pay it off.

☐ **Complete the table on the next two pages, using your account statements from the last 3 months.**

Example Montly Credit Card Cost at 15.75% APR

ACCOUNT	BALANCE		INTEREST RATE					MONTHLY COST
Credit Card	$1,000	Ⓧ	15.75%	Ⓧ	.01	÷	12	=

What Your Debt Costs You Each Month

Include any Auto Loans, Student Loans, Credit Cards, or other Similar Debt

1 **Account Name:**   **Balance:**

INTEREST PAID (First Month)	INTEREST PAID (Second Month)	INTEREST PAID (Third Month)	LAST 3 MONTHS' INTEREST	AVERAGE MONTHLY COST
+	+	=	÷ 3	=

2 **Account Name:**   **Balance:**

INTEREST PAID (First Month)	INTEREST PAID (Second Month)	INTEREST PAID (Third Month)	LAST 3 MONTHS' INTEREST	AVERAGE MONTHLY COST
+	+	=	÷ 3	=

3 **Account Name:**   **Balance:**

INTEREST PAID (First Month)	INTEREST PAID (Second Month)	INTEREST PAID (Third Month)	LAST 3 MONTHS' INTEREST	AVERAGE MONTHLY COST
+	+	=	÷ 3	=

4 Account Name: _____ Balance: _____

INTEREST PAID (First Month)	INTEREST PAID (Second Month)	INTEREST PAID (Third Month)	LAST 3 MONTHS' INTEREST	AVERAGE MONTHLY COST
+	+	=	÷ 3	=

5 Account Name: _____ Balance: _____

INTEREST PAID (First Month)	INTEREST PAID (Second Month)	INTEREST PAID (Third Month)	LAST 3 MONTHS' INTEREST	AVERAGE MONTHLY COST
+	+	=	÷ 3	=

6 Account Name: _____ Balance: _____

INTEREST PAID (First Month)	INTEREST PAID (Second Month)	INTEREST PAID (Third Month)	LAST 3 MONTHS' INTEREST	AVERAGE MONTHLY COST
+	+	=	÷ 3	=

Total Monthly Cost of All Accounts: _____

Strategies to Eliminate your Debt

Revolving debt - in other words, debt that you carry on your credit cards - comes at a significant cost. Most credit cards charge high interest rates on balances that are carried over into the next month, and you want to avoid these types of fees and penalties at all costs.

Start with Your Smallest Balance

One of the most effective methods for paying is starting with your credit cards – specifically, the ones that have the highest interest and lowest balance. The intended result is a snowball-like effect of paying down more and more of your balances over time.

First, make sure to stay current on all of your accounts and pay them on time in order to avoid costly fees and penalties. Then, dedicate as much of your remaining budget as possible to paying down the card with the lowest balance.

Once you've paid off your first card, use the money you were paying as a minimum monthly payment on this account and combine it with another to pay down your next lowest balance. Over time, this method should drastically reduce what you owe on your cards. Until you've eliminated your credit card balances, keep current on your fixed-term loans, like your mortgage or car payment, as usual: they usually charge a much lower interest rate.

Consolidate Your High-Interest Credit Card Balances With a No-Interest Transfer

Another method that might save you money and make it possible to pay down your debt more quickly is to consolidate your credit cards – especially those with high interest rates – to a credit card with zero percent interest. Many credit card companies offer a promotional rate on balance transfers, which can buy you some extra time. Just be aware that often, they also charge a one-time balance transfer fee for a percentage of the balances. There isn't interest charged on this amount, either.

Be wary of lines of credit that can be used to consolidate your debt. Many lenders will extend a loan to people with low credit scores, but sometimes at an interest rate in excess of 30%.

The cost of attending a 4-year college is estimated to rise to

$262,000

for a child born in 2013[13]

Invest and Insure

While you're working to improve your credit score and reduce your family's debt, you should also start setting more ambitious saving goals. In the short term, you're not likely to realize any significant gains - but this is an important first step to establishing saving habits early.

Saving for College

If college costs continue to balloon at the current rate, you'll need to invest in order to help cover tuition when your small scholars graduate from high school. There are many tax incentives that can help you out: for example, a 529 plan grows tax-free and you can spend from the account with a penalty, provided you use the funds to pay for qualified educational expenses. Some states offer tax deductions for participating in their plans, too, saving you even more when you file your taxes.

Saving for Retirement

The sooner you get started on building a retirement account, the larger it will be when you're ready to retire from work.

Because this account will compound, if you invest it with a moderate level of risk tolerance, it's likely to grow significantly over time. Like college savings, there are also many tax incentives for contributing to retirement accounts, too. Set a goal of investing 15%: of what you make in either a traditional or Roth IRA.

Long-Term Savings

Even though you've got your $1,000 emergency fund, it's important to save even more for medium to long-term expenses that might come up unexpectedly. Set a goal to save at least three to five months of your family's take-home pay, which can help avert disaster in the event of a major medical emergency or accident.

Insurance Coverage

As a result of the Affordable Care Act, many people who were not insured prior to 2012 have obtained health insurance; however, millions more still are underinsured or uninsured altogether—

at a significant risk to their families. While the law requires you to obtain auto insurance (if you drive) and health insurance (if your employer doesn't provide it), there are other types of coverage that aren't required, but necessary for your family's financial health.

Life Insurance

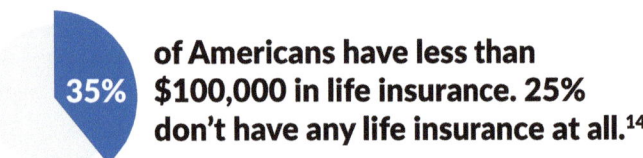

35% of Americans have less than **$100,000 in life insurance. 25% don't have any life insurance at all.**[14]

In case tragedy strikes, it's important to have life insurance. A good policy won't by any means replace you, but it will help keep your family out of the financial trouble that will almost certainly arise from catastrophe. Most life insurance policies also offer a benefit in the case of terminal illness: an important feature that will help your family. Consider purchasing a policy for seven to ten times your annual salary—and purchase it as early as you can in life. The younger you are, the lower the fixed rate you'll be able to obtain.

Homeowner's Insurance

If you own a home, a homeowner's insurance policy is a must: many banks require a policy when they issue a mortgage loan, and with good reason. Not only is a homeowner's policy important for protecting the external structure and contents of the home, it also covers your personal liability as a property owner, in the event someone is injured on your property. Additionally, many insurance policies can have a jewelry rider that can insure valuables like jewelry. If you live in a place where there might be earthquakes or flooding, be sure to look into extra coverage, as these disasters are not typically covered by most basic policies.

Renter's Insurance

If you're renting property, it's important that you don't underestimate the importance of having renter's insurance. Renter's insurance is designed to cover the cost of replacing your personal belongings if they're damaged or stolen - but it also helps cover the cost of accommodations if your unit becomes uninhabitable. It's usually not very expensive, either.

Problems Paying Medical Bills Among Low and Middle-Income Non-Elderly Adults[15]

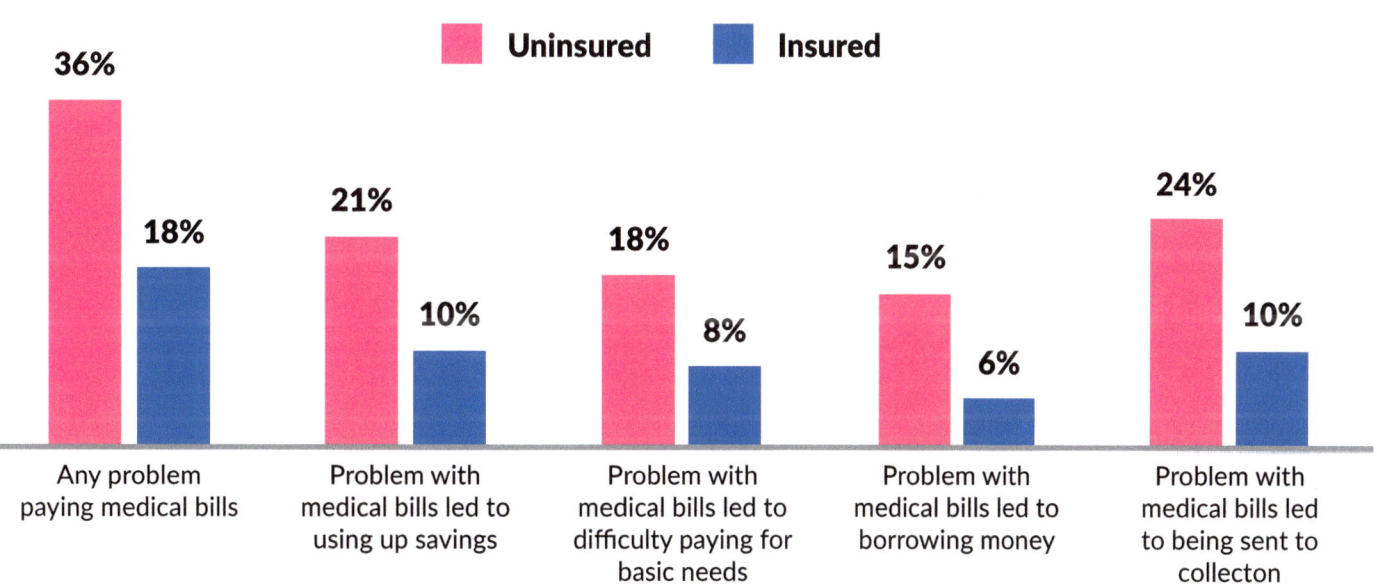

V View Your Accounts Often

Even if you've managed to build a healthy savings account, pay down your debt, and invest in your future, you'll still need to carefully monitor your finances. Whether you're going through paper statements or transactions on your bank's website, it takes time to check in on your accounts and you'll need to set time aside to do it regularly. Mint.com is a reputable website/resource run by Quicken (the same company that makes TurboTax) that helps you view all of your account information in one place. Once you've linked your accounts, Mint keeps them updated, and gives you alerts and advice to help manage your transactions.

Automated Payments

Most of the hassle caused by the many different due dates can be eliminated by setting up automatic payments and withdrawals for your bills. But even if you've eliminated the need to remember to pay each bill individually when it's due, you'll still need to carefully monitor the transactions to ensure they're accurate.

Alerts and Notifications

Many banks (as well as cell phone, TV, and Internet service providers) have applications for your smartphone that let you log in and manage your accounts. Most also offer the option to sign up for text message alerts on your phone, which can be extremely helpful in case you accidently forget to pay a bill or overdraw your account. If you'd like to access this information all in once place, a website like mint.com allows you to set customized alerts.

☐ **Automate your bill payments and withdrawals.**

☐ **Create an account on Mint.com and link your financial accounts to see everything in once place.**

☐ **Sign up to receive text message or email alerts from your bank or other service providers.**

E Enjoy Your Financial Freedom

The final principle of **THRIVE** includes strategies for enjoying the results of the hard work you've done to manage your family's finances.

Give Generously

Once you've succeeded in establishing healthy budgeting and spending habits, it's important to be generous. Donate to charities, give thoughtful gifts, and surprise people once in a while. If a kind heart isn't reason enough to adopt this practice, there's research that suggests that people who are most connected to their personal networks accumulate the most wealth.

Pursue Your Passion

A benefit of having a stable pattern of spending and saving is being able to afford to spend some money on the things you're passionate about. Sometimes, your hobby can be worth money, too - which can definitely help with your family's finances. Even if your crocheting doesn't help you collect millions, you'll still be free to spend a little extra money doing something you truly enjoy.

Take a Family Vacation

Some of the best memories you'll have with your children are when you take time away from work to make memories together. Be deliberate in leaving your work behind for a few days or weeks every year, and do something fun together as a family. If you've worked hard to manage your finances responsibly, it's important to enjoy the product of your hard work as a family.

CONCLUSION

After taking the time to analyze your spending, stash away some money in case of an emergency, and get your budget in order, you're likely already in a better place than where you started. As you build your credit score, you'll have access to better rates, rewards programs, and—perhaps most importantly—the flexibility to adjust your monthly spending with a broader financial picture in mind.

Just like there are no guarantees with your health, there's no certainty in finance, either. But just as regular exercise, a healthy diet, and routine care can help you avoid many health problems, carefully monitoring your accounts, establishing healthy spending habits, and saving money will help you avoid falling into a financial hole.

For every dollar that you spend, you get something in return. Sometimes, that "something" is of little value, lasts for only a moment, or depreciates quickly. Other times, that "something" becomes an asset, increases in value, or has a long-term payoff. Ultimately, there probably isn't any "something" that will be more valuable than raising your family. Just as your body needs food to eat in order to grow and thrive, your family needs money to pay for things like meals, shelter, and clothing. But money can't purchase the important moments parents have with their children, cure a terminal illness, heal a chronic disease, or buy you extra hours.

It is essential to keep your financial goals in perspective: it's not what your family achieves, but how your family approaches the challenge of working to establish responsible spending and saving habits—together—that will help you thrive financially and ensure a secure future for your children.

APPENDIX

LOGIN AND PASSWORD INFO

If you're hesitant to store all of your usernames and passwords online, you can keep them here. This is also a good reference in case you need to have someone log in and pay a bill in an emergency situation.

ACCOUNT NAME	ACCOUNT NUMBER	PASSWORD	NOTES

ACCOUNT NAME	ACCOUNT NUMBER	PASSWORD	NOTES

A CRASH COURSE ON CREDIT

One of the most fundamental aspects of thriving financially is understanding your credit score and knowing how to manage it.

The three major credit reporting bureaus, Experian, Equifax, and TransUnion, all report financial information to make up what's known as a FICO score, which is used to approve or deny credit card applications, determine how much credit is extended, or determine your rate and qualify you for a mortgage or auto loan.

Your FICO score impacts your finances more than you might think: it determines your ability to qualify for a cellular phone contract, transfer a utility bill into your name, apply to be a tenant at a rental property. Your credit score impacts the rate you pay for automobile insurance, the deposit you'll be expected to put on file with Satellite TV providers, and possibly even your ability to use a company credit card your boss may issue to you at work.

Fortunately, there are many tools that are currently available that simplify your credit report and can help you monitor and manage your credit rating.

The most important thing to keep in mind is that your credit score builds over time. It is designed to be a reflection of your ability to spend within your means and pay what you owe consistently - and there aren't any quick fixes. However, just as missed payments and overuse damage your credit score, each on-time payment or reduced balance improves it. The next five steps are things that, over time, will help you improve your score.

12-18 MONTHS

How long experts say it will take to see a significant improvement in your credit score[16]

HOW YOUR CREDIT SCORE IS CALCULATED[16]

30% AMOUNTS OWED
It's not necessarily bad to borrow and owe money - but overusing your credit cards will be a drag on your score.

35% PAYMENT HISTORY
Do you make your payments on time? Your reputation as someone who pays their bills on time is the most important factor in determining your credit score.

15% LENGTH OF CREDIT HISTORY
It won't hurt if you've have limited use of credit cards or haven't had them for a very long time, depending on how the rest of your credit report looks.

10% CREDIT MIX
Your credit mix is a blend of your credit cards, long-term and fixed-rate loans, and department store cards.

10% NEW CREDIT
If you don't have a strong credit history and you open several new accounts in a short period of time, statistically this signals a great risk to your lenders.

Appendix C:

SOURCES

1. "American Household Credit Card Debt Statistics: 2015 - NerdWallet." NerdWallet Credit Card Blog. NerdWallet, n.d. Web. 17 Jan. 2016.

2. "At Last, a Proper Recovery." The Economist. The Economist Newspaper, 14 Feb. 2015. Web. 18 Jan. 2016.

3. "To Pay Off Loans, Grads Put Off Marriage, Children." WSJ. The Wall Street Journal, n.d. Web. 17 Jan. 2016.

4. "The Cost of Raising a Baby." Parenting. Parenting.com, n.d. Web. 18 Jan. 2016.

5. W. Bradford Wilcox, Joseph Price, and Robert I. Lerman. "Strong Families, Prosperous States: Do Healthy Families Affect the Wealth of States?" American Enterprise Institute. Web.

5. http://www.creditcards.com/credit-card-news/ownership-statistics-charts-1276.php

6. "An Average ER Visit Costs More than an Average Month's Rent." Washington Post. The Washington Post, n.d. Web. 21 Jan. 2016.

7. http://www.nextadvisor.com/blog/2012/03/22/what-should-my-car-insurance-deductible-be/

8. http://usnews.rankingsandreviews.com/cars-trucks/best-cars-blog/2013/04/Auto_Repair_Costs_are_on_the_Rise/

9. http://money.usnews.com/money/personal-finance/articles/2014/04/30/the-hidden-costs-of-moving

10. http://money.usnews.com/money/personal-finance/articles/2013/09/18/5-creative-ways-to-cut-airfare-costs

11. "Learn How Much It Costs to Repair a Furnace." 2016 Furnace Repair Costs. Home Advisor, n.d. Web. 21 Jan. 2016.

12. "How Much Does Water Heater Installation Cost?" Angie's List. Angie's List, 20 Apr. 2012. Web. 21 Jan. 2016.

15. College Cost

14. http://www.bankrate.com/finance/insurance/money-pulse-0715.aspx

15. http://kff.org/uninsured/fact-sheet/key-facts-about-the-uninsured-population/

16. http://www.myfico.com/crediteducation/whatsinyourscore.aspx